Tarot Spreads of the Greek Gods

Anthony Whitman

and

Jessica Tiderman

Sage & Hawthorn Print, LLP

Printed in the United States of America

First Printing, 2014

ISBN 978-0-9960638-1-4

Sage & Hawthorn Print, LLP
www.sagehawthorn.com

Dedication

To our wonderfully fabulous children -
Thank you for cooperating with us and each other
and for tolerating us while we worked on this book.

Table of Contents

Introduction

In 1911, Arthur Edward Waite published a book titled The Pictorial Key to the Tarot. In that book, A.E. Waite gives the following brief introductory description about the Celtic Cross: *"I offer in the first place a short process which has been used privately for many years past in England, Scotland, and Ireland."* He then follows with a chapter on how to use this spread with tarot cards. It is amazing how a paragraph and one chapter can have such a huge influence on a century of tarot reading.

Since then, the Celtic Cross has been the main staple of most tarot readers. Unfortunately, most of the new spreads developed are variations of three and five card spreads which are very limited by their past-present-future designs. We believe that this situation is entirely unacceptable for a tool as rich and intricate as tarot. Thousands of decks have been created and the intuition that goes along with reading the tarot has advanced significantly. If new spreads are developed, it does not mean that the Celtic Cross will become dead and forgotten. Variety and versatility are foundations of our humanity, and those traits are easily applied to tarot.

These spreads are meant to appeal to all types of tarot readers: from religious minded individuals, who wish to accompany the reading with a spiritual ritual, to the secular readers, and anyone in-between. Prior to the spreads is a page with secular associations for those wish to strip the readings down to their most basic parts. While we use the tarot in a very spiritual manner, we understand it is not the same for everyone else. There are secular readers, as well as readers from all religions and denominations. These spreads are designed to be used by anyone, from all walks of life.

The first part of the spread is an excerpt of a Homeric or Orphic hymn. There are two exceptions. The first is the Chiron spread, for which no Orphic or Homeric Hymn exists; he is not mentioned in any others as well. The second is the Column of the Gods spread. This spread was not based on a deity, but on a distinctly Greek architectural pattern, the Corinthian column. The hymn sets the initial context of the spread and can also serve as an homage for the spiritual reader. Following the hymns are brief descriptions of the deity. The descriptions are then followed by explanations the symbol's use and its relation to the spread.

All spreads are based upon a symbol of a Greek deity that lends both its meaning and physical shape to the spread. The meaning of the symbol gives the spread its purpose, while the symbol itself gives shape to the spread. We wanted the spreads to be more than patterns on a table with strict linear placements. We wanted them to be total worlds in and of themselves. Symbols reach a person on the deepest level, this is the level where tarot intuition thrives.

Most of the artwork chosen to accompany these spreads was taken from the areas of classical statuary, pottery paintings, and mosaic artwork. Where the appropriate related piece of artwork was not to be found, supplemental sources such as Roman and Modern sources were used. For Hera's Peacock Feather, a new photograph was used.

Specific meanings of the cards themselves or discussions of the use of reverse meanings are not in this book. We feel that there are already numerous 'little white books' that explain the meaning of each card. It is the reader's choice whether or not to use reverse cards and their implications in these spreads. These readings were not designed to exclude that type of card meaning within the spread.

Although this book is called Tarot Spreads of the Greek Gods, it does not imply that all Greek deities were considered. An opposite line of thinking was taken and the Greek deities chosen were the ones deemed most relevant to today's tarot readers. That is how we chose the Greek deities that were to get their own spreads – instead of what was more popular in ancient Greece.

Secular Associations
(Forces of...)

These aren't meant to be the strict ancient Greek mythological interpretations. They have been inspired to coincide better with the modern processes of tarot.

Zeus: kingship, law, fate, order, ruling, royal husband.

Hera: queenship, marriage, domestic order, royal wife.

Athena: crafts (weaving), wisdom, counsel, civil judgment (court of law).

Hermes: trade, business, communication, travel, writing.

Poseidon: the sea, rivers, horses, floods, subconscious.

Aphrodite: love, beauty, physical pleasures, relationships.

Artemis: hunting, childbirth, wild animals, female divination, sudden change in the female realm.

Apollo: sudden change in the male realm, music, art, male divination, and sometimes death and disease.

Eros: lust, trickery, infatuation, impulse.

Hades: death, ghosts, funeral rites, the underworld, reincarnation.

Persephone: spring, life, maidenhood, unwilling participation.

Demeter: agriculture, herbalism, plants, seasons.

Dionysus: wine, revelry, festivals, holidays.

Hephaestus: fire, crafts, blacksmithing, trade-skills.

Hestia: hearth, cooking, passions, desires, domesticity.

Ares: war, aggression, defense, defiance.

The Muses: spiritual artistic expression.

Themis: law, order, and civil conduct.

Asclepius: healing, health, medicine.

Pan: wilderness, far off places, mystic realms.

Helios: solar attributes.

Selene: lunar attributes.

Hecate: shadows, the unknown, last resorts, and unusual circumstances.

Chiron: teaching, tutoring, guidance, discipline, rewards.

iii

Court Card Associations

For Greek Deities

King of Swords: Zeus
Queen of Swords: Hera
Knight of Swords: Athena
Page of Swords: Hermes

King of Cups: Poseidon
Queen of Cups: Aphrodite
Knight of Cups: Artemis
Page of Cups: Eros

King of Pentacles: Hades
Queen of Pentacles: Demeter
Knight of Pentacles: Persephone
Page of Pentacles: Dionysus

King of Wands: Hephaestus
Queen of Wands: Hestia
Knight of Wands: Apollo
Page of Wands: Ares

SPREADS

Column of the Gods

(Corinthian)

Image courtesy of WikiMedia Commons.

To See Which Gods (Forces) are the Most Present

| 13 | 14 | 15 |

⟨11⟩   ⟨12⟩

| 9 | | 10 |

| 7 | | 8 |

| 5 | | 6 |

⟨3⟩   ⟨4⟩

| 1 | | 2 |

As we mentioned in the Introduction, this spread differs from the rest of the spreads in this book. There is no hymn, and the design is not based on a sacred symbol associated with a Greek deity. The design is based on a distinctly Greek architectural pattern, the Corinthian column. The spread is meant to be an introductory one.

For this reading, the court cards are to be separated from the deck and used by themselves, while the rest of the deck is to be put aside (see earlier court card associations table.) This spread can have two contexts. For those querents who know which gods (divine forces) are the most present in their life, this reading is to determine which other gods or forces want their attention right now. For those querents who aren't aware of the most powerful forces in their life (or their patron/matron deity), this spread is to determine what the most powerful forces are in their life presently. The card positions are to be read in a very linear fashion: the cards at the bottom have the least presence in the querent's life, while the cards at the top have the most presence in the querent's life.

Card Meanings:

1, 2: These cards represent the forces that are barely present, or have barely impacted the querent's life.

3, 4: These cards represent the forces that have a passing interest in the querent's life.

5, 6, 7, 8, 9, 10: These cards represent the forces that the querent has worked with in the past, or forces that have had a noticeable impact in their life.

11, 12: These cards represent the forces that are secondary in focus in the querent's life currently.

13, 14: These cards represent the forces that are primary in impact and importance in the querent's life. They can be viewed as the matron and patron.

> (If there is only one male card in placements 11-15, then that card may be viewed as the patron of the querent; and vice-versa for only one female card.)

3

15: This card represents the main force, or main deity, in the querent's life. It may also mean the force that most desires the querent's attention.

The experienced reader will notice that there is one card leftover from the sixteen court cards. This card is the zero card, to be put on a corner of the area where the reading is taking place. This card is not part of the spread proper, but it is still important. This card represents the force that is ambivalent, indifferent, or angry in certain contexts, in the querent's life.

Lyre of the Muses

Image courtesy of WikiMedia Commons.

For Transcending the Mundane and Inducing a More Spiritual Mindset

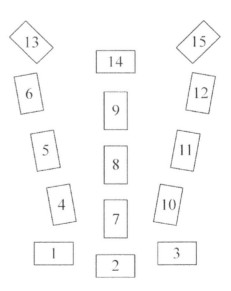

From the Muses, Apollo, and Zeus I will make my beginning of song. For it from the Muses and Lord Apollo who shoots from afar that men upon the earth are singers and skilled with the lyre, and from Zeus that men are kings.
    - Homeric Hymn 25
    Crudden

Everyone knows that music holds great power. It can bring back memories, inspire spiritual states of mind, and transport us to other places and times. The skills of the Muses could even influence the moods of the Gods, as they were known to sing during the banquets on Mount Olympus. This is the secret of the Muses for this spread - they can take us to higher and more spiritual places.

This reading is to discover how the Muses can help us transcend the everyday mundane and secular, to unlock the more spiritual parts of our minds. It is even possible to delve into which of the nine methods of each Muse is the most powerful for the querent.

At the bottom of the spread are the more 'settled' states of mind, where the querent operates day to day. The middle part of the reading is the 'fountain', or 'spring', of the Muses, from where the divine inspiration comes from. The top of the reading are the 'airs', or realms of the leaders of the Muses: their mother Mnemosyne, their father Zeus, and their artistic leader Apollo.

Card Meanings:

1, 2, 3: These are the three main focuses and concerns of the querent's everyday affairs. The mundane frames of mind.

4-12: The Well/Spring: These are the methods of the muses. They determine how that specific Muses' realm affects you. Each card may also explain the querent's attitude towards their respective spheres. These placements summarize each Muses' relationship with the querent.

4: This is the card of Calliope, the muse of poetry.

5: This is the card of Urania, the muse of astronomy (or astrology if the querent chooses).

6: This is the card of Polyhymnia, the muse of religious hymns (more involved specific spiritual matters, or prayer).

7: This is the card of Erato, the muse of erotic poetry (or sexual expression).

8: This is the card of Terpsichore, the muse of song and dance.

9: This is the card of Melpomene, the muse of tragedy.

10: This is the card of Thalia, the muse of comedy.

11: This is the card of Euterpe, the muse of lyric poetry.

12: This is the card of Clio, the muse of history.

13: This card is the air of Mnemosyne. It reveals how or what you remember of spiritual things from your past.

14: This card is the air of Zeus. It reveals your highest spiritual concerns.

15: This card is the air of Apollo. It shows how you are to use that frame of mind, the purpose of your personal spiritual gifts.

Scales of Themis

Image courtesy of WikiMedia Commons.

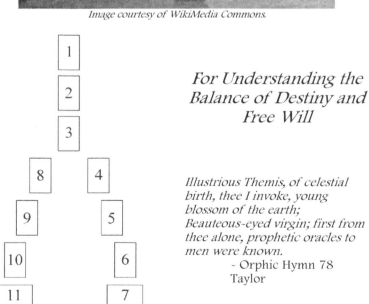

For Understanding the Balance of Destiny and Free Will

Illustrious Themis, of celestial birth, thee I invoke, young blossom of the earth; Beauteous-eyed virgin; first from thee alone, prophetic oracles to men were known.
~ Orphic Hymn 78
Taylor

To the Greeks, there were the laws made by people and laws made by Zeus and the other gods. Themis was the deity whose role it was to dispense and maintain these divine laws. She was oftentimes more associated with oracles than swords and scales. There is no hard date on the adoption of the scales as one of her symbols; it may have been very recent. However, I feel that it is a useful adaptation to give Themis' spread a very in-depth context.

As the Goddess of Rule and Law, Themis can represent the position of humanity to either choose to obey boundaries out of their control, or to disregard the laws and rules of city, state, and Gods (cosmos). This spread is for finding a balance of fate and free will; in relation to the spreads of pure fate (the Scepter of Zeus), and pure choice (Artemis'/Apollo's Arrow).

Card Meanings:

1, 2: These cards are the situation, problem, or choice in question. It lets the querent know what is being balanced on the scales. It is the complex and layered situation in the querent's life that is being influenced by the scales.

3: This card is the pivot of the scales, the key to the reading. This card shows what choice is to be made, or path that has to be followed, depending on which sides of the scale weigh more heavily upon the querent. This card may also be read as the final outcome if the querent decides to keep the sides of the scales evenly balanced in their life, and may be turned over last. The reader may ask the querent if they wish this card to be turned over first or last. The reader may also ask the querent which side of the spread is to be read first, the choice side or the fate side.

4 - 7 represent the choice side of the spread, while cards 8 - 11 represent the fate side of the spread.

> 4, 5, 6: These cards are the choices you can make in regards to the pivot card. They can also be clues that you have already chosen to follow your own free will in relation to card 3. (The querent can influence what is shown in these cards.)

7: This card is the result that will occur if you decide to follow the free will side of the scale.

8, 9, 10: These cards are the situations that fate has placed on your path. They may also be clues that you are living your life according to what fate has ordained for you.

11: This card is the result that will occur if you are the type of person who lets fate decide what happens in your life. Some will also see this view as a choice within itself, but in this context you will not fight fate, and be more accepting.

Caduceus of Asclepius

Photo by Michael F. Mehnert, courtesy of WikiMedia Commons.

In Regards to Spiritual Health

With Asclepius, plague-healing son of Apollo, my song begins. King Phlegyas' child, bright Koronis, gave birth on the Dotion plain, to this great joy for humans who charms ill pangs away.
> ~ Homeric Hymn 16
> Crudden

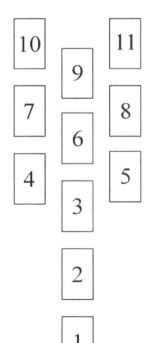

Asclepius was the son of Apollo who was killed by Zeus because his healing powers were so great that he could bring the dead back to life. Zeus felt that he was violating divine law by giving life back to the deceased. After his death, Asclepius was placed as the constellation Ophiuchus. His symbol was technically a simple staff with a snake entwined around it, and not the caduceus associated with today's medical associations.

As Asclepius was mostly associated with healing, this spread is also to delve into the querent's health. However, this reading is not to be taken literally. For medical health issues, please see a qualified practitioner. The health referred to in this reading is strictly spiritual. There is also considerable leeway as to what order the querent may wish to read the cards, i.e. 3, 6, and 9 first – or 3, 4, and 5 first.

Card Meanings:

1-2: These cards represent the overall health of the querent. These cards can be read as two separate issues, or read as parts of one whole issue.

3, 6, 9: These cards represent the problems of spiritual health concerning the querent. These cards may also be read as three different issues, or as one issue.

4, 7, 10: These cards represent the what, how, or why of the cause affecting the spiritual health issues in cards three, six, and nine.

5, 8, 11: These cards represent the cures, or what will heal the issues present in cards three, six, and nine.

Branch of Chiron

*For Guiding Students
and Children*

Photo by Giovanni Dall'Orto, courtesy of
WikiMedia Commons.

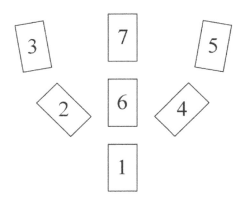

Chiron was the half-brother of Zeus, Poseidon, and Hades. They shared the same father, although Chiron had a different mother. This centaur was responsible for teaching Asclepius in the healing arts. Teaching medicine to his pupils was just one of his many talents. Chiron also mentored Achilles (of the Trojan War), and Jason (leader of the Argonauts). There are many images of him hunting and training with weapons. He was also depicted as traveling with a multi-pronged branch that had the spoils of the hunt on it. I believe that this symbol is a worthy one for a teacher who was entrusted to rear some of Greek myth's most revered heroes.

The context of this spread is for those looking for a balanced hand in the training, education, disciplining, etc., of children or students. It may be used for those in difficult situations, or for general early preparation.

Card Meanings:

1: This card is the handle of the branch. It represents the personality type needed in regards to authority.

2, 3: These cards represent methods of discipline, judgment, punishment, etc. – that are too harsh.

4, 5: These cards represent methods of rewards, gifts, or praise that are too kind.

6, 7: These cards represent the tempered approach, methods of discipline or praise that fit the situation and the person in question best.

The three pairs may be read together as parts of one situation, or as separate answers.

Reed-Pipes of Pan or the Nymphs

Photo by Sharon Mollerus, courtesy of WikiMedia Commons.

For Seeking Help from Spirit Guides

| 1 | 2 | 4 | 7 |

| | 3 | 5 | 8 |

| | | 6 | 9 |

| | | | 10 |

Concerning Hermes' beloved offspring speak to me, Muse, that goat-hooved, two-horned lover of clamor who roams through meads of woodland together with the nymphs whose nature it is to dance. Down peaks of rugged rock they tread and call on Pan, the squalid god of pasture with splendid hair, who owns each snowy ridge, the mountain's summits and rocky ways.
- Homeric Hymn 19
Crudden

Pan was not one of the Olympians, and was most likely a more minor god. He was important enough to warrant his own selection in the Homeric Hymns. Today, Pan is a very popular character from the Greek myths. His realm was that of the shepherds and hunters that roamed the wilderness, along with the nymphs he was fond of chasing.

Pan, the satyrs, and the nymphs were also occasionally attendants to the gods – so this spread is for seeking advice from the querent's spirit guide, totems, animal guides, or ancestors. When shuffling, the querent may think of an already known spiritual helper. If the querent does not know of one, the first card may show who or what that entity is. As with the Arrow and Chariot spreads, the Pan title for the males, the Nymph for females; unless chosen otherwise.

Card Meanings:

1: This card represents the overall sense of what the entity in question is doing. It can range from their mission as the querent's guide, their current magical focus, their purpose in helping, or many other ventures. It may also be a clue to the identity of the helper.

2, 3: These cards are what the entity wishes to tell or communicate to the querent.

4, 5, 6: These cards represent the forces affecting both the querent and the entity. They can also describe the bond that the querent and the entity have.

7, 8, 9, 10: These cards represent four weaknesses that the querent and the entity need to work on together.

Hoof Prints of Pan

*For Recovering or
Interpreting Dreams*

*Photo by Sharon Mollerus, courtesy of
WikiMedia Commons.*

> *Throned with the Horai (Seasons), Bacchanalian Pan, goat-
> footed, horned, from whom the world began; in endless
> dance and melody divine. In thee a refuge from our fears we
> find, those fears peculiar to humankind.*
>   - Orphic Hymn 11
>   Taylor

As Pan lived in the wilds and the edges of civilization, this spread utilizes his presence as an excellent source to explain and illuminate things that are mysterious to us - beyond normal borders or boundaries, as well as the edges of our own psyche. These things can be hidden paths, sacred springs, or overgrown groves. Dreams can also serve as a refuge for the dreamer. The specific context of this spread is for explaining remembered dreams - the hidden or overgrown paths of our minds. Like the Three Torches of Hecate, this spread can be laid out three times, if the ability to recover more than one dream is desired.

Card Meanings:

1: This card is the context, or description of the overall sequence of events in the dream.

2, 3: These cards represent what the dream means.

4, 5: These cards represent actions that the querent should take in reference to the dream. These actions may be solving a problem that the dream brought up, or seeing a situation through that the dream was describing.

Chariot of Selene and Helios

Image courtesy of WikiMedia Commons.

Celtic Cross Style Spread

1	2
3	4

5

6

10

9 8 7

Begin now, Muse, Kalliope, daughter of Zeus, a hymn to the beaming Sun, whom cow-eyed Euryphaessa bore to the child of Earth and starry Sky.
        - Homeric Hymn 31
        Crudden

Of the long-winged Moon give utterance, sweet-spoken Muses, to sing, Young maiden daughters of Kronos' son Zeus, who are skilled in song. That light that in heaven is plain to view is whirled to earth from her deathless head, and vast is the splendor, rising slow, of that light as it shines.
        - Homeric Hymn 32
        Crudden

In Greek myth, the sun and moon had their own identities and names. The sun was Helios, his sister Eos was the dawn that signaled his arrival. Selene was the other sister, the moon. These three siblings were not Olympians, but of the older generation of Titans. Helios and Selene drove the sun and moon across the sky with their own respective chariots.

This spread was designed for querents who still like the more general Celtic Cross type readings. Like Artemis' Arrow spread, this spread has a 'momentum' connotation with it; as a driver on his or her chariot. However, in addition to a general reading, there are also solar and lunar attributes that can be taken from the spread as well. The specific name used with this spread can depend on the sex of the querent. If the querent is a male, it is the Chariot of Helios, and the Chariot of Selene for females. However, if the querent is a female and asks for the solar reading, the Chariot of Helios may be done for her; and vice-versa for a male making the same request.

Card Meanings:

1, 2: These cards represent the view of the chariot driver, or in this case, the querent. For Solar, readings these are that which is seen, illuminated, gives light, almost in an overbearing sense - as one who stares at the sun. For Lunar readings, these are that which is hidden, shrouded in darkness, that which we only see in the night - with the moon as light.

3, 4: These cards are what relaxes the querent.

5, 6: These cards are what pulls/drives the querent, by choice or not.

7, 8: These cards represent that which the querent is seeking.

9, 10: These cards are what hold the querent back.

Arrow of Artemis or Apollo

Image courtesy of WikiMedia Commons.

To Make a Choice when the Situation is Known

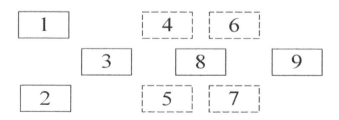

Sing, Muse, of Artemis, sister of him who shoots from afar,
the virgin huntress reared with Apollo... Her horses' thirst
she slakes in Meles' reed-choked stream, and quickly then
drives through Smyrna her car of pure gold to Klaros where
vines abound. There Apollo is sitting, god of the silver bow,
awaiting his archeress sister, the goddess who shoots from
afar.
> - Homeric Hymn 9
> Crudden

Artemis and Apollo were the twin children of Leto and Zeus. Apollo was the god of music, prophecy, disease, hunting, and archery, among many other things. Artemis had more defined roles, that of huntress, and the protector of children, virginity, and maidenhood. One of their most powerful myths is that of Queen Niobe. This mortal woman boasted that since she had seven sons and seven daughters, she was greater than Leto. Leto and her twin children did not react to this boast well, as Artemis took her bow and killed the seven daughters, while Apollo swiftly killed the seven sons.

Even though Artemis and Apollo were very complex deities, their arrows would strike down anyone at any time and were symbolic of the swiftness of their decisions. This reading is to present the querent with four clear choices in regards to a very specific question. Whereas other readings also deal with choices, this reading deals with one choice out of different available options. The arrow symbol was chosen to show where the momentum from a choice may take the querent. If the querent is a female, the reading is called Artemis' Arrow. If the querent is a male, then the reading is Apollo's Arrow. When the querent is shuffling, it would be helpful to think of an already known situation in which guidance in decision-making is needed.

Card Meanings:

1, 2: These cards represent the past (decisions, actions) that brought the querent to the choice that they have to make.

3: This card is the present situation for the querent, which calls for a choice to be made.

(Cards 1 through 3 can be described as the situation that necessitates that a choice be made.)

4, 5, 6, 7: These cards are the four options from which the querent selects one as their choice after each card is explained.

8: This is the one card that the querent selected from the cards 4 through 7, and is the choice that will be made.

(This card placement on the spread is for illustration – as the actual card placed there will be one of the cards from 4, 5, 6, or 7. When the solution card is chosen it is placed on position 8, the other three are removed from the spread. It is designed so that the final product looks like the 'arrow'.)

9: This is the final outcome, what will happen when the choice (card eight) is made.

Hearth of Hestia

Image courtesy of WikiMedia Commons.

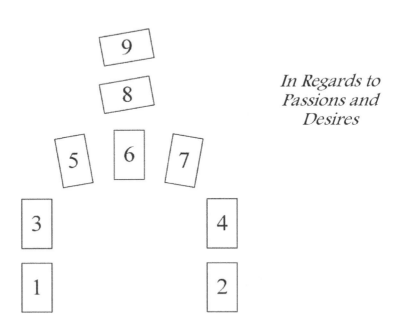

In Regards to Passions and Desires

Hestia, you who at holy Pytho bestow your care on the sacred abode of the lord, Apollo who shoots from afar, the locks of your hair are always dripping with liquid oil. Enter this house, your heart at one with Zeus the wise, enter, and grant to my song your favoring grace besides.
      - Homeric Hymn 24
      Crudden

Hestia did not have as large a collection of myths as many of the other Olympians. She was one of the three sisters to Zeus, along with Demeter and Hera. Every Greek household had an altar, sometimes a room, devoted solely to this goddess. She was included in the prayers and praises of many household activities. Her importance was a given, even if not talked about as much as the other more popular deities.

As Hestia is the Goddess of hearth and home, this spread represents the concerns of inner hopes, wishes, dreams, and desires, as well as familial duties, maternal care, and household matters. This reading is to dwell on the passions and desires of the heart and contented soul.

Card Meanings:

1, 2: These cards are the deepest concerns of the person, almost at a subconscious level, that gives the querent purpose in day to day activities. These cards can also be desires and passions that have already been satisfied.

3, 4: These cards are the more active concerns of the person, what they think about and focus on more often. These cards can be what actively drives the querent day to day.

5, 6, 7: These cards are the flames on the hearth, they represent the true desires that the person wishes to focus on. The context is usually something new that the person wishes to bring into their life, since it is a flame burning within their heart.

8, 9: These cards are the smoke from the flame. Sometimes smoke can be black and noxious, or it may be sweet and clear. If the person fanned the flames of cards 5, 6, 7, then 8 and 9 reflect what may happen.

Three Torches of Hecate

Image courtesy of WikiMedia Commons.

To Determine What Type of Magic is to be Used (Or Stance to be Taken)

For nine days then queenly Deo wandered across the earth, a flaming torch in each hand, and neither ambrosia touched nor sweet-tasting nectar in grief, nor with bath-water splashed her flesh. But when the tenth time upon her the radiant Dawn had shone, then she was met by Hecate, holding a light in her hands.

~ Homeric Hymn 2
Crudden

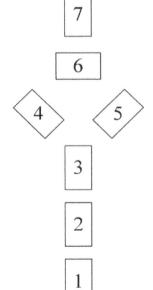

Hecate was the goddess of a myriad of forms of magic. While many like to focus on the dark or unknown qualities of this deity, it is important to remember that it was Hecate that aided Demeter in the search for her daughter Persephone after she was kidnapped by Hades. Hecate was known for carrying torches in the night, and used this power to aid Demeter in her frantic search.

This reading is to alert the querent to magical or spiritual situations that require attention, and the magic to be used for each. The form of 'magic to be used' should be defined by the querent (for example, if a wand card is drawn, it could signify means of fire and passion, as in burning a boon). It does not have to be a literal context, unless the querent wishes it to be. It can be a 'stance to be taken' as well, i.e., actions for resolving a conflict.

This card layout can be used up to three times in the spread, even though only one is shown here.

Card Meanings:

1, 2, 3: These cards describe the situation that needs the querent's attention. These cards are to be read as parts of a whole.

4, 5, 6: These cards represent the type of magic to be used to address the situation. The cards may be read as a whole (as in the components of a spell, aspects of a situation), or individually (as in steps to take.)

7: This card will tell the querent how they will know when or if their working was successful.

For those who may want further spiritual clarification on the types of magic that can be used, these associations may be helpful:
Pentacles: herbalism, offerings, libations.
Cups: alchemy, new mixtures.
Wands: spells, workings.
Swords: ceremonies, rituals, projects.

Demeter's Sheaf of Wheat

Image courtesy of WikiMedia Commons.

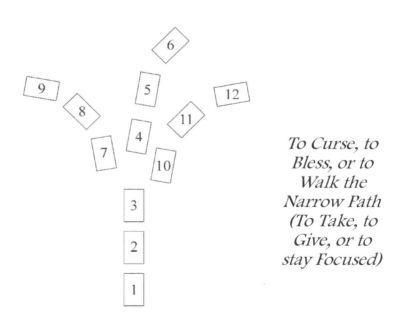

To Curse, to Bless, or to Walk the Narrow Path (To Take, to Give, or to stay Focused)

Demeter, Bringer of Seasons, Bestower of Splendid Gifts...
      - Homeric Hymn 2
      Crudden

Demeter was one of the three sisters of the first generation of Olympians, along with Hera and Hestia. She was popularly known as the goddess of bountiful harvests and a host of agricultural matters. After her daughter Persephone was abducted by Hades, she wandered the earth and let the fields and groves become barren. Humankind would have perished, had not Zeus ordered Hades to release Persephone.

While Demeter was associated with fertility and the harvest - what is not usually focused on is her ability to bring ruin down upon mankind when she is angry. In this aspect, she is the both giver and taker of the sustenance of men and women. The purpose of this reading is to focus on the giving and taking aspects of Demeter.

Card Meanings:

1: This card represents the querent's state of being, or position, that this reading directly affects.

2: This card represents the magnitude of the three possible effects (branches or wheat sheaves) on the querent. It may hardly affect their day-to-day activities, or it may have a life-altering effect on their entire spiritual outlook.

3: This card represents the overall situation or outlook that the three branches deal with, in respect to the querent.

4, 5, 6: These cards are the neutral cards of the reading. This is the path that Demeter (or an authority figure) set before the querent that will be the way of things if neither her ire nor favor is gained.

> 4: This card represents the overall pattern of the things that Demeter has set before the path of the querent.

> 5: This card represents how the querent will navigate (or is navigating) this path.

6: This card represents the outcome of the querent's path if neither ire nor blessing is gained.

7, 8, 9: These cards are the 'curse' of Demeter. They represent what will happen if her ire is gained.

7: This card represents the action that gained (or will gain) Demeter's ire.

8: This card represents that curse itself.

9: This card represents the outcome of the 'curse' on the querent.

10, 11, 12: These cards are the 'blessing' of Demeter. They represent what will happen if her favor is gained.

10: This card represents the action that gained (or will gain) Demeter's favor.

11: This card represents the blessing itself.

12: This card represents the outcome of the 'blessing' on the querent.

Anvil of Hephaestus

Image courtesy of WikiMedia Commons.

In Regards to Careers, Crafts, and Hobbies

5

6   8   10   12

7   9   11

3   4

1   2

Sing, you clear-voiced Muse, of Hephaestus renowned for craft, who with bright-eyed Athena taught splendid works to humans on earth – they had before been dwelling in caves on the mountains like beasts, but now, knowing works through Hephaestus renowned for his skill, with ease, till the year brings its end they live in comfort within their own homes. Come now, be kindly, Hephaestus, grant us prowess and wealth.
- Homeric Hymn 20
Crudden

Hephaestus was the craftsman who made all sorts of wonders for the Gods. He made the homes they lived in; armor for Thetis' son, Achilles; and the metal net that caught his wife Aphrodite having an affair with Ares.

As Hephaestus was the god of blacksmithing and crafting, this spread is for the same use. In respect to arts and the Lyre of the Muses spread, this reading has more choice involved, and can be related to more mundane matters. It must be kept in mind that many people's careers are related to their passions and artistic expressions.

Card Meanings:

1, 2: These cards represent the querent's current job, career, or main form of artistic expression.

3, 4: These cards represent the querent's personal view on cards 1 and 2. For example, they may or may not be content to the situations present in cards 1 and 2. These cards may also explain why they are or are not content.

5: This card represents the querent's natural, or favorite, artistic talent.

6, 7, 8, 9, 10, 11: These cards represent or summarize the effects of their career on the world around them.

12: This card represents why the querent has this talent or skill.

Tongs of Hephaestus

*For Handling
Delicate (Hot)
Situations*

*Sculpture by Herman Wilhelm Bissen
Photo by James Steakley, courtesy of WikiMedia
Commons.*

7

8

6

5

2

4

1

3

Strong, mighty Vulcan, bearing splendid light, un-wearyed fire, with flaming torrents bright: Hear, blessed power, to holy rites incline, and all propitious on the incense shine: Suppress the rage of fires un-wearyed frame, and still preserve our nature's vital flame.
   - Orphic Hymn to Vulcan, the Roman Hephaestus
   Taylor

One of the myths of Hephaestus was that he fell from Olympus for nine days and when he landed he became lame. In light of this he was not deemed as attractive as the god, Ares, who caught the eye of his wife, Aphrodite. Hephaestus suspected that Ares and Aphrodite were having an affair in his bed while he was away crafting things for the gods. He created a net that caught them 'in the act', and Hephaestus then invited all the other gods to come and get a good laugh at the misfortune of the trapped lovers.

As this famous myth demonstrates, Hephaestus had a unique way of handling delicate situations. It is fitting to use his tongs as a symbol for a spread of the same use.

Card Meanings:

Cards 1, 2, 3, 4 are the two situations that are causing the conflict, and each set is to be read as two cards describing one situation (events up to the conflict).

> 1, 2: These cards represent the first of the two situations, in regards to what is causing the conflict. (One side of the story.)

> 3, 4: These cards represent the second of the two situations, in regards to what is causing the conflict. (The other side of the story.)

5, 6: These cards represent the present or actual conflict in question.

7, 8: These cards represent the solution(s) to the conflict, or ways to solve it. They can read as two parts of one solution, or each card separately.

Seashells of Aphrodite

Image courtesy of WikiMedia Commons

*For Advice on
Building
Relationships*

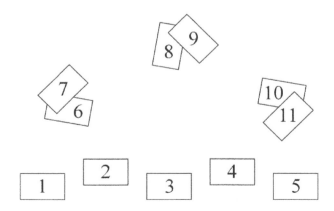

Speak to me, Muse, of golden Aphrodite's works, the
Cyprian's – she who sends sweet desire on the gods, and
subdues the tribes of mortal men, the birds that fly through
the air, and all the many wild beasts that are nurtured by
land and sea...
- Homeric Hymn 5
Crudden

There are conflicting accounts of the parents of Aphrodite. Some said that she was born of the sea foam, other say that she is the daughter of Zeus and Dione. However she was born, she became the goddess of love, beauty, and sexuality. There is a very large collection of myths surrounding this deity, with a variety of themes and plots.

As Aphrodite was the goddess of love, this spread is for someone seeking an outlook on a relationship with a lover. The three pairs of cards represent seashells (with two halves open but still connected); while the five base cards represent the waves of the sea. Whereas the Rose of Aphrodite Spread deals with how to fix a relationship, this spread is for further building on an already good relationship or remembering the healthy aspects of it.

Both of these Aphrodite spreads can be used for more than one querent at the same time.

Card Meanings:

1, 2, 3, 4, 5: These cards are the foundations of the relationship. They can be things solved in the past, as well as good choices made.

6, 7, 8, 9, 10, 11: These three pairs represent things that the couple can work on to complement each other and strengthen the relationship. The top card on these pairs is the querents, and also means they have to take the first step; as they are the ones receiving the reading. Each pair is a separate situation. The even cards are to be placed first.

Rose of Aphrodite

In Regards to Weak Areas in a Relationship

Photo by Clio20, courtesy of WikiMedia Commons.

6

5   7

4

3

2

1

I will sing of that beautiful goddess who wears a crown of gold, revered Aphrodite, who owns on all Cyprus surrounded by sea each circling head-dress of towers. There strong Zephyr's moist breath through crashing waves conveyed her, amid the soft foam, to shore.
     - Homeric Hymn 6
     Crudden

The rose may seem a cliché or little used symbol in the artwork of Aphrodite, but I believe it was as relevant then as it is today. The Greeks did associate the rose with this deity, although not as prominently as seashells and mirrors.

As the other Aphrodite spread, this is for the querent to discover the weaker aspects of a relationship with a lover - so that those aspects can be worked on. Whereas the seashell spread is for improving on an already strong relationship, the rose is for fixing a possibly broken relationship.

Card Meanings:

For this spread, the Major and Minor Arcana are to be separated. The Major Arcana are used for cards 1, 2, and 3; while the Minor Arcana are used for cards 4 through 7.

1: This card represents the querent.

2: This card represents their lover.

3: This card represents the overall status of the relationship

4, 5, 6, 7: As these cards are laid down, the reader is to focus on what is missing. If there is an abundance of pentacles, and no cups – then emotion is missing from the relationship. If all high numbers are present, then the relationship is too complicated. These are just two examples, and the reader may further develop the explanation of these four cards. Some cards may also be read as self-explanatory if no pattern of missing cards is discernible.

Vine of Dionysus

Photo by Shakko, courtesy of WikiMedia Commons.

To Seek or Quell Distractions

With the god who has ivy hair, Dionysus who roars out loud, the splendid son of Zeus whom glorious Semele bore, I begin to sing. He was reared by nymphs whose tresses are fair: from the lord his father they took to their bosom and fostered with care this child in the hollows of Nysa.
      - Homeric Hymn 26
      Crudden

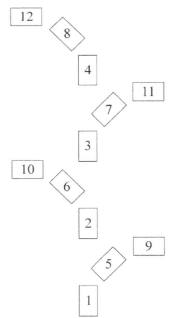

Dionysus was a later addition to the pantheon of the Greeks. Even though his domain was related to the vine, wine, and revelry – the theaters were also dedicated to him. At the front of the theater was an altar to Dionysus, while his priests were seated at the front. This deity had the distinction of having a mortal mother (Semele, his father was Zeus,) while not being simply a demigod.

As Dionysus was the god of wine and revelry, this spread is based on a symbol of a vine. This spread is for focus or stress relief. This reading is to determine what should be, or what is, distracting you. Things that should be distracting you are to be read in a positive light, like how to let off some steam. Things that are distracting you can be read as negative, as in things that are causing stress.

Card Meanings:

For this spread, cards that are reversed may be read as the negative distractions, as opposed to right side up as the positive ones. This spread presents four separate instances of positive or negative distractions. Cards 1, 5, 9 are the first situation; 2, 6, 10 are the second situation, etc.

1, 2, 3, 4: These cards are the distractions themselves, and may be interpreted by the querent (possibly afterward) as either being good or bad.

5, 6, 7, 8: These cards are the steps needed to be taken; either to bring about the needed distraction, or to get rid of it. These cards are where a querent may have lots room interpreting what is or could be distracting, what can be ignored, what can be focused on, etc.

9, 10, 11, 12: These cards are the results that will happen, if the proper steps (5, 6, 7, 8) are taken.

Persephone's Pomegranate

*To Balance the Elements, the Underworld,
Olympus (Heaven), and Earth*

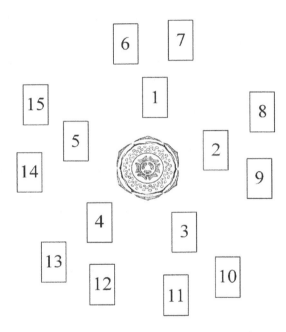

Center image courtesy of WikiMedia Commons.

*In this way he spoke, to the joy of Persephone shrewd in
thought. She quickly leaped up in delight, but secretly,
glancing round, he gave her to eat a pomegranate's honey-
sweet seed, so that there by revered Demeter the dark-robed
she would not forever stay.*
        - Homeric Hymn 2
        Crudden

Persephone was the daughter of Zeus and Demeter, and the unwilling bride of Hades. She was out picking flowers when the King of the Underworld abducted her and took her to his realm. Hades at first had permission from Zeus to take this maiden for his bride, but after Demeter withheld all crops from humankind to the point of famine, Zeus reversed his decision. Unfortunately for Persephone, she had already eaten fruit in the realm of Hades, a pomegranate, and had to stay with him the same number of months as the seeds she ate. Accounts differ as to how many seeds she ate, and therefore how long she had to reside with Hades. The rest of the time Persephone could spend where she pleased.

As Persephone spent some of the year in the Underworld and some of the year on the Earth – for this spread she is used for the context of balance. More specifically, she is the balance of the elements, since she spends time in different realms. This reading is to determine what is lacking in the querent's life in the sense of the elemental qualities. There are the five points of the pentagram corresponding to the traditional associations, with an additional ten cards (two for each of the points). For the specific positions of the elements on the pentagram, Greer's Encyclopedia of the Occult was used. It is at the discretion of the querent whether cards 1 through 5 are read first; or each elemental grouping (card 1, then 6 and 7, and so forth). For this spread, the major arcana should be separated from the rest of the cards and both parts shuffled separately. Deal from the major arcana for cards 1 through 5 and from the minor arcana for the rest. The inner circle of major arcana shows what needs to be brought in to add more or to keep the current balance. The outer minor arcana show the querent how that is to be accomplished.

Card Meanings:

Cards 1, 2, 3, 4, 5 can be read as overbearing strengths and hindering weaknesses at the same time.

1: This card is what is out of balance in the querent's element, qualities, and associations of Spirit.

2: This card is what is out of balance in the querent's element, qualities, and associations of Water.

3: This card is what is out of balance in the querent's element, qualities, and associations of Fire.

4: This card is what is out of balance in the querent's element, qualities, and associations of Earth.

5: This card is what is out of balance in the querent's element, qualities, and associations of Air.

6, 7: These cards will show the querent how to balance the element of spirit in their life.

8, 9: These cards will show the querent how to balance the element of water in their life.

10, 11: These cards will show the querent how to balance the element of fire in their life.

12, 13: These cards will show the querent how to balance the element of earth in their life.

14, 15: These cards will show the querent how to balance the element of air in their life.

Staff of Hermes

Image courtesy of WikiMedia Commons.

For Enhancing Communication

Of Hermes, Kyllenian god and slayer of Argos, I sing, who over Kyllene reigns and Arkadia rich in flocks, the immortals' speedy messenger. Maia gave him birth, Atlas' daughter, having joined in love with Zeus, being worthy of reverence.
> ~ Homeric Hymn 18
> Crudden

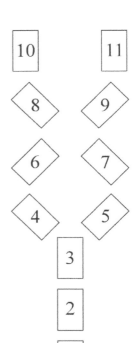

Hermes was another very complex Greek god. Zeus was his father by a shy nymph named Maia. He was the patron deity of merchants, businessmen, and travel. As well as that realm of influence, he escorted the dead to Hades, and also served as messenger to the gods. In some myths he also plays the role of a trickster god, for example when he stole Apollo's cattle and walked his footsteps backwards so that he couldn't be followed to his hideout. In artwork, he is shown with either with the caduceus or a staff with an unusually crafted top.

One of Hermes' strongest influences was over communication. This spread is for determining the strong and weak areas of the querent's communication skills.

Card Meanings:

1: This card represents the querent's basic overall skill of listening.

2: This card represents the querent's basic overall skill of understanding what was heard. In essence, how well does the querent absorb what is told to him/her.

3: This card represents the querent's basic overall skills and views with how they communicate back to others, or reciprocate. It also may deal with how the message was received by others.

4, 5, 6, 7: These cards represent areas where the querent needs work, or further development with their communication skills.

8, 9, 10, 11: These cards represent areas where the querent's talents lie in regards to communication.

Shield and Spear of Ares

Image courtesy of WikiMedia Commons.

In Regards to Defense and Aggression

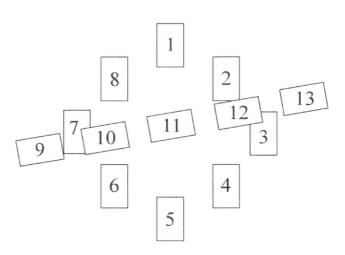

Ares surpassing in might, who weigh the chariot down, who wear a helmet of gold and possess a spirit of strength, shield-bearing savior of cities, clothed in armor of bronze, whose mighty hand unwearied wields a spear that is strong...Pay heed, you ally of mortals, giver of flourishing youth, and from on high shed down a gentle light on our life, and martial strength to give me power to drive from my head the bitter taint of cowardice, power to thwart with my mind the soul's deceitful impulse, and power besides to hold back the fierce might of spirit that pricks me to enter chill strife...
- Homeric Hymn 8
Crudden

Ares had a very specific function - he was the god who thrived during war. While Athena was more interested in the strategy of battle, Ares was more about the raw violence of the actual fight. There were mixed feelings from the other gods about his place among the Olympians. Nevertheless, war was sometimes inevitable, as was his role in it. He was also one of the few children that Zeus and Hera had together.

As befitting the god of War, this spread is for recognizing and defending against brute attacks on the querent. The circle part of the spread is for defending, and the spear is for counterattacks and further defense.

Some of the inspiration for this spread was taken from accounts of an early 19th century French cartomancer, Marie Anne Lenormand. It is rumored that the court cards in her readings represented specific types of people we may encounter daily. I decided to expand upon that idea and create four social spheres in our modern daily lives that can be equated to the four suits, with the court cards representing important people in our lives from those spheres. Pentacles are work and career. Swords are friends and peers. Wands are past and current romantic relationships. Cups are family members.

The top part of the shield illustrates what or who is currently attacking the querent. The bottom part of the shield reveals an attack that has just ended. On the two sides of the shield are vulnerabilities of the querent that may be assaulted in the future. It is also possible that any major arcana on the shield may be karmic forces, past actions, that have come back to afflict the querent.

Card Meaning:

1: This shows who or what is attacking the querent. If it is not a court card, it still reveals another method of attack; which provides another clue to the identity of the attacker.

2,3: These cards show the methods of the attacker from card 1.

4: This card shows who or what just finished attacking the querent. It is to be read in the same fashion as card 1.

5,6: These cards show the methods of the attacker from card 4. It is read the same as cards 2 and 3.

7, 8: These cards show personality traits or actions that may leave the querent open and vulnerable to possible future attacks.

9, 10: These cards are the best methods of defense for what is revealed in card 4.

12, 13: These cards are the best methods, or allies, for the defense of card 1.

11: This card is the grip of the spear. It represents the best personal trait, or ally, for defending against all attacks in general. It may also work for all examples on the shield.

Aegis of Athena

To Discover and Confront Fears

Photo by Marie-Lan Nguyen, courtesy of WikiMedia Commons.

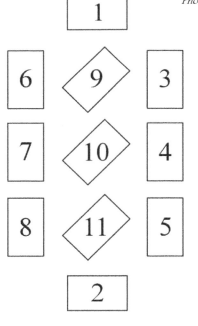

With Pallas Athena, protectress of cities, my song begins, with that fearsome goddess who cares with Ares for warlike works...
   ~ Homeric Hymn 11
   Crudden

Athena was a favorite among the Greeks, as attested to by the name of one of their greatest cities, Athens. She ruled over many functions: defense, civilization, wisdom, crafts, arts, and many more. Due to some very unusual circumstances, she was born out of Zeus' forehead, even though Metis (the personification of wisdom), was her mother. Most statues show her with some assortment of weapons, (shield, spear, and helmet) and also with the Aegis on her breast. Some accounts say that this special breastplate was made with fearsome snakes; others that it is the head of Medusa herself.

Even though Athena was the Goddess of crafts, wisdom, and war - the framework of this spread focuses on her Aegis. To look upon Athena took great bravery. The context of this spread is to confront one's fears.

Card Meanings:

1, 2: These cards are the causes of the fears (of cards 9, 10, 11).

3, 4, 5, 6, 7, 8: These cards are the tools that the querent can use to face their fears.

9, 10, 11: These cards are the deepest fears of the querent.

This spread is to not to be treated in the traditional manner. The cards are not to be turned face-up in the same linear way that they were laid down. Cards 9, 10, 11 are to be picked out last, at random, from inside the deck, akin to an illusionist telling someone to 'pick a card, any card'. This method is to represent the chaos and irrational manner that fear sometimes manifests itself.

Steps:
- ❖ The querent shuffles normally.
- ❖ The querent lays out cards 1 through 8 face-down as in a normal reading.
- ❖ The querent picks three cards at random from anywhere in the deck.
- ❖ The last three cards are picked out and put in the 9, 10, and 11 card places, face-up, and are the first cards to be read.

❖ Cards 1 and 2 are then turned over and interpreted in the reading.
❖ Cards 3 through 8 are turned over and interpreted.

Once all the cards are face up, the querent has six ways (cards 3, 4, 5, 6, 7, 8) that they can deal with the three fears. The querent can place those three 'fear cards' on top of the three 'solution' cards of their choice.

Helm of Athena

Image courtesy of WikiMedia Commons.

To Seek and Receive Wisdom and Advice

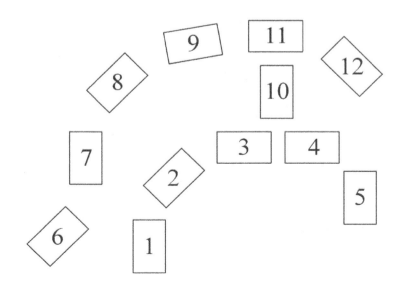

With Pallas Athena, that glorious goddess, my song begins,
who is bright-eyed, rich in craft, who has an implacable
heart, the virgin revered, protectress of cities, possessor of
strength, Tritogenes.
　　　- Homeric Hymn 28
　　　Crudden

Being the daughter of Zeus and Metis, Athena was the goddess of wise counsel and wisdom. This spread is for the seeking and giving of these same attributes. The context of this symbol has two layers. The first layer (bottom of the helm) is based on sight, i.e. what is behind, not seen and forgotten; as opposed to right in front of the querent's sight, and at the forefront of their thought, which could be clouding or blocking their vision. The sight context of the spread is to help understand the querent's thought processes. The second layer, the crest on top of the helm, concerns the advice and wisdom aspect of the reading and builds off of the thoughts and views of querent from the first layer.

Card Meanings:

1: This card represents concerns that have been forgotten about and left far in the past.

2: This card represents matters that the querent has set to the rear and perhaps should pay more attention to. The querent may want more time and effort devoted to them.

3, 4: These cards represent concepts or situations that the querent has grasped and is successful in helping with others. The querent has devoted much time and effort to these ideas.

5: This card represents a subject or conflict that blinds the querent, or blocks their vision. The querent may start to devote less time and effort dealing with this.

6: This card represents topics that the querent does not have much experience with, and should not offer advice to anyone.

7, 8: These cards represent general areas of expertise that the querent should seek out advice for, as they are also somewhat lacking in this type of experience.

9: This card represents matters that the querent has a little experience with, and that which they can offer advice to others, hesitantly.

10: This card represents the influence of Athena, or the forces of wisdom, in their decision-making or counseling methods. For example, the types of situations that the querent always seems to be negotiating, or in the middle of (also learning curves and obstacles meant to overcome.)

11: This card represents the gift of Athena, or the forces of wisdom, to the querent. It is the skills given to use on card 10.

12: This card represents the topics that Athena wants the querent to seek out and advise upon. These are situations where the querent is wisest and can help others.

Trident of Poseidon

For Delving into the Subconscious

Photo by Marie-Lan Nguyen, courtesy of WikiMedia Commons.

6

12

9

5

11

8

4

10

7

3

2

1

Concerning Poseidon, that mighty god, I begin to sing, who stirs the earth and murmuring sea, the lord of the deep, who over Helicon rules and spacious Aigai too. In twain the gods divided, Shaker of Earth, your share of honor – to be the tamer of horses and savior of ships.

    - Homeric Hymn 22
    Crudden

Poseidon was the brother to Zeus and Hades, and when the three realms of the Greek cosmos were divided up and chosen by lot, this deity received the sea. He ruled the depths of the ocean, the power of the waves, and would cause earthquakes when angered. Poseidon was also associated with many Greek cities, even though he dwelt in the ocean, and even competed with Athena for the patronage of Athens.

The symbol of Poseidon's power was the trident, a spear with three points. He used this weapon to shatter rocks, call forth or subdue storms, and shake the earth. For this spread the sea is equated to the subconscious. There are three depths of the sea or subconscious in this reading, and it has a much more a secular design than others in this book. Self-awareness of the subconscious is the key of the spread.

Card Meanings:

Cards 1, 2, and 3 are issues in the varying depths of the querent's subconscious.

> 1: This card represents the bottom of the sea, or concerns that reside in the querent's deepest subconscious.

> 2: This card represents the middle depths of the sea, issues that are neither at the surface nor the bottom of the querent's subconscious.

> 3: This card represents the surface of the sea, affairs just on the brink of the querent's subconscious.

Cards 4, 5, and 6 represent how the querent should handle or react to these issues.

> 4: This card corresponds with the issue in card 1.

> 5: This card corresponds with the issue in card 2.

> 6: This card corresponds with the issue in card 3.

Cards 7, 8, and 9 represent what will happen if the querent confronts these issues, or 'brings them forth from the depths of their subconscious'.

7: This card corresponds with the issue in card 1.

8: This card corresponds with the issue in card 2.

9: This card corresponds with the issue in card 3.

Cards 10, 11, and 12 represent what will happen if the querent decides to keep these issues suppressed, or buried within their subconscious.

10: This card corresponds with the issue in card 1.

11: This card corresponds with the issue in card 2.

12: This card corresponds with the issue in card 3.

Throne of Hades

Photo by AlMare, courtesy of WikiMedia Commons.

*To Seek the
Other Half of
the Soul
(Reincarnation
Spread)*

Hades was the god of the underworld, where the souls of Greek myths went after death. It is sometimes confusing that the Greeks used the name 'Hades' to mean both the god, and also the name of the realm he presided over. A person who died could both go to Hades to meet him, or go to Hades to dwell there. The way there was often complicated and involved many other deities. Thanatos was the actual god of death, who caused a person's life to cease. Hermes guided the soul to the gates of the underworld. When arriving, the deceased soul crossed the first river of Hades, called Acheron, by riding in the boat of Kharon. The existence and purpose of the rivers in Hades is the focus of this spread. There were five rivers that were known in Greek society. These were: the River of Forgetfulness - Lethe; the River of Sorrow - Acheron; the River of Hate - Styx; the River of Wailing - Kokytos; and the River of Fire - Phlegethon.

When a soul entered Hades, they had to pass over these rivers before they could be reincarnated. Encountering the River of Forgetfulness would explain how most people who believe in reincarnation cannot remember anything from their past lives. However, according to a later Greek writer named Pausanias, in some mystical traditions, there was a secret sixth river that initiates could drink from, the River of Mnemosyne. Encountering this river could bring back memories from past lives.

It is the possibility of the existence of the River of Mnemosyne in mind that this spread draws its inspiration from. This reading is to give the querent the option of glimpsing into a few past life memories and then deciding if they do indeed want to keep those memories, or know more about the past lives in question. When shuffling, the querent should think about how recent of a past life they may wish to examine. Some people may want to glimpse into one of their first lives, others may want to know about the most recent one.

Card Meanings:

1: This card is to show the querent how they may ask permission from Hades to obtain this knowledge; since the reading is basically bending the rules of his realm.

Cards 2 through 6 symbolize the Reed of the River of Lethe. They deal with the past life that the querent has chosen to examine.

2: This card reveals how mature the soul of the querent was at the time of the past life in question. It is very hard to think in linear terms when dealing with how many times and at what frequency a soul may have been reborn. It is not assumed that every soul has been constantly reborn like an assembly line.

3, 4, and 5: These cards describe the concerns, focuses, and activities of the past life in question.

6: This card explains how the querent can re-forget these memories if they are not happy with the results. Not everyone may want to remember a past life that was painful or tragic.

Cards 7 through 11 symbolize the Reed of the River of Mnemosyne. They can help instruct the querent on the responsibilities that come with these newfound memories.

7: This card reveals why the querent wishes to know about this past life in particular.

8: This card helps the querent realize whether or not they should have these memories.

9 and 10: These cards give instruction on how more memories from this past life may be obtained, if the querent is satisfied with the description of the past life in question.

11: This card gives the querent clues as to methods they can use to keep these past life memories permanently.

12: This card shows how the querent can give thanks to Hades for allowing this knowledge to be gained.

Tiara of Hera

In Regards to Fertility of All Types

Image courtesy of WikiMedia Commons.

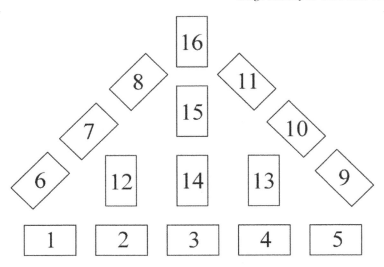

*O royal Hera, of majestic mien, aerial-formed, divine, Zeus'
blessed queen, throned in the bosom of cerulean air, the race
of mortals is thy constant care. The cooling gales thy power
alone inspires, which nourish life, which every life desires.
Mother of showers and winds, from thee alone, producing all
things, mortal life is known: all natures share thy
temperament divine, and universal sway alone is thine, with
sounding blasts of wind, the swelling sea and rolling rivers
roar when shook by thee. Come, blessed Goddess, famed
almighty queen, with aspect kind, rejoicing and serene.*
     - Orphic Hymn to Hera
     Taylor

Hera is one of the most misunderstood Olympians. She resided over marriage rites, birth, and fertility. However, many myths show her chasing down Zeus' multiple loves with great fury. Some of the tales are cruel, like that of Io, where Hera had her turned into a cow and tormented by a gadfly while she roamed the earth. It must be remembered that Hera was one of the few Olympians that was married, and unlike Aphrodite - Hera was not renowned for having an affair in her husband's bed. For all of the myths of her jealous anger, there seem to no myths of her having trysts with mortals or other gods. In fact, the myth of Ixion tells of a man who tried to seduce Hera, but she told Zeus of the attempt and he punished this person severely by binding him to a wheel of torture.

Since Eileithyia, the goddess of childbirth and midwifery, was a daughter of Zeus and Hera, it is logical that Hera could also be consulted on how succeed in relationships in general. As the queen of the gods, it would be her who would wear the crown, or in this case, the tiara. This spread is for determining what is needed to conceive; whether it be a literal need or a figurative need. Even though this spread is centered on woman-man relationship, it can easily be adapted to two males or two females. Even in the figurative sense of 'conceiving' a new spiritual family – two friends can be substituted on either side of the tiara.

Card Meanings:

1, 2, 3, 4, 5: These cards represent favorable signs that a couple may start trying to conceive.

6, 7, 8: These cards represent steps, or situations, that the female needs to address before conception can occur.

9, 10, 11: These cards represent steps, or situations, that the male needs to address before conception can occur.

12: This card represents situations that may hinder the female from participating in the conception.

13: This card represents situations that may hinder the male from participating in the conception.

14, 15: These cards represent situations that the female and male must accomplish together for conception to occur.

16: This card represents the stage or sign that signals conception has occurred.

Hera's Peacock Feather

In Regards to Goals and Domestic Order

Photo by Morgan Burke © 2013

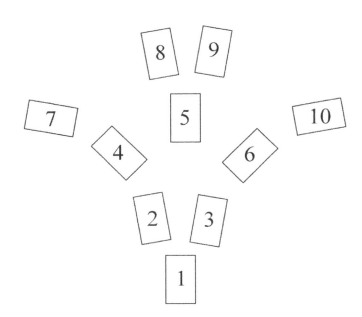

Of Hera I sing, whose throne is golden, whom Rhea bore, the immortal Queen, beyond compare in beauty of form, the glorious sister and spouse of Zeus who thunders loud, whom all the blessed gods upon tall Olympus rank in dread and honor as equal to Zeus whom thunder delights.
- Homeric Hymn 12
Crudden

Some of Hera's myths show her assisting mortals in great adventures, such as the Argonauts' quest for the Golden Fleece, and siding with the Greeks during the Trojan War. The queen of the Olympians had the power to set things into motion that helped mortals, or to see mortal plans through to their end. This spread is for delving into any steps needed to see a goal through. The querent may think of a desired event when shuffling or laying the cards, and then the cards may map out the course to that end. The querent may also have a clearer mindset and let the cards take a more active role in determining their goals. It may also be assumed that Hera (forces of domestic order) will be aiding the querent in an indirect way.

Card Meanings:

1: This card represents the current state of affairs in respect to the querent's desired goal, or may indicate the goal itself if it is not known

2, 3: These cards represent the immediate concerns that need to be addressed in respect to the desired goal.

4, 5, 6: These cards represent the short term concerns that need to be addressed in respect to the desired goal.

7, 8, 9, 10: These cards represent the long term concerns that need to be addressed in respect to the desired goal.

Lightning Bolt of Zeus

Following Divine Decree

Image courtesy of WikiMedia Commons.

1

3

2

4

5

6

8

7

9

As king of the gods, Zeus was in charge of the laws and destinies of both mortals and gods. He expressed himself through thunderclouds and lightning. In the Iliad, Zeus tells all the other Olympians that they may not assist their favorite mortals or join in the Trojan War at all. Later, Hera and Athena try to defy his order, but Iris commands them to return, and they cannot disobey. Who knows how the Trojan War would have turned out if Zeus had allowed the other Olympians to assist their favorite heroes on both the Trojan and Greek sides?

For us mere mortals, the desire to follow the will of the gods, the divine decree, should be of utmost importance. Therefore, this reading is based on the symbol of Zeus' will in action, the flash of lightning. This spread is for delving into the querent's knowledge of, or adherence to, the laws of the gods (universe). It can be gleaned from the context of the reading if the querent is adhering to the path that Zeus has laid down before them. As the lightning bolt starts in the clouds and ends on the earth, so this spread is to be read in the same fashion. The terms divine decree, law, rule, and governance may all be used interchangeably. This decree is meant to be specific to the querent, as opposed to the global worldly sense. For more secular querents, Zeus may be interchangeably used with the terms the cosmos or the universe.

Card Meanings:

1: This card represents the decree, or the will of Zeus on Mount Olympus, that affects or has the most impact on the querent.

2, 3: These cards represent the situation on Mount Olympus that created the need for the decree. It can explain the meaning behind the decree, or how it will benefit the Gods.

4, 5, 6: These cards represent the signs that card 1 is being enforced on earth. For example, if the querent sees these signs, then they are following what was decreed in card 1.

7, 8: These cards represent the situations on earth, that match the situation on Mount Olympus in the macro-microcosm relationship sense – that card 1 is meant to address. This can be interpreted as how the decree is benefiting the querent or how the decree can be used by the querent.

9: This card represents the decree, in card 1, as it manifests on earth in relation to the querent.

Scepter of Zeus

Image courtesy of WikiMedia Commons.

To Discover One's Fate or Destiny

Of Zeus I will make my song, of the best and greatest of gods, the far-seeing sovereign from whom fulfillment comes. It is he who to Themis murmurs wise words while inclining towards him she sits. Be gracious, Kronos' greatest, most glorious, far-seeing son.
- Homeric Hymn 23
Crudden

6

4   5

3

2

1

Just as Hera had a bad reputation of chasing down Zeus' lovers, the king of the gods was frequently shown finding new and clever ways to have affairs. Aside from these myths, Zeus was far seeing and privy to information that even many gods were not aware of. He knew how the Trojan War would end.

For the focus of this spread, Zeus' title of 'Moiregetos', Leader of the Fates, is used. This reading is for the discovery of the querent's fate and destiny. As opposed to many other readings where there are many different types of choice, this spread has no choice. It lets the querent know the length of the thread that has been spun for him/her by the Fates. The terms cosmos or universe may be interchanged with Zeus or the Gods. This spread is not for the light-hearted.

Card Meanings:

1: This is the card of Clotho. It tells the querent of their main trait in the eyes of the Gods. (The type of thread chosen.)

2: This is the card of Lachesis. It will tell the querent of the length of time (their thread) and the path that they will walk.

3: This is the card of Atropos. It will tell (warn) the querent of the stage when they will know their thread is to be cut.

4: This card will tell the querent how card 1 will affect those around them.

5: This card will tell the querent how card 2 will affect those around them.

6: This card will give the querent signs that their thread is about to be cut or that they are ready for it to happen, depending on the querent's personal beliefs about fate and destiny.

Pediment of the Gods

Photo by Tilemahos Efthimiadis, courtesy of WikiMedia Commons.

To Discover the Gifts of the Gods

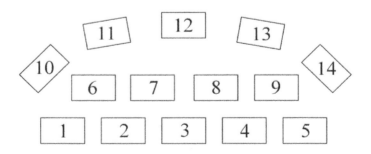

From the Muses, Apollo, and Zeus I will make my beginning of song.
For it is from the Muses and lord Apollo who shoots from afar
That men upon the earth are singers and skilled with the lyre,
And from Zeus that men are kings. But blessed is the man
Who is loved by the Muses: sweet is the voice that flows from his
lips.
Farewell to you, children of Zeus, and honour this song of
mine.
But I will call to my mind both you and another song.
　　　- Homeric Hymn 25
　　　Crudden

In the Greek myths, there was a contest between Athena and Poseidon as to whom a city should be named after. Athena and Poseidon both offered gifts to the people, and the people were to decide which gift was more useful. Poseidon offered the horse, whereas Athena offered the olive tree. In the spirit of that contest, this spread is for determining each of the Olympian Gods' gift to the querent. It is up to the querent to interpret the time span of the gifts in question.

Card Meanings:

1: This card is the gift of Aphrodite.

2: This card is the gift of Demeter.

3: This card is the gift of Hera.

4: This card is the gift of Persephone.

5: This card is the gift of Athena.

6: This card is the gift of Artemis.

7: This card is the gift of Dionysus.

8: This card is the gift of Hermes.

9: This card is the gift of Ares.

10: This card is the gift of Hestia.

11: This card is the gift of Poseidon.

12: This card is the gift of Zeus.

13: This card is the gift of Hades.

14: This card is the gift of Hephaestus.

Bibliography and Suggested Reading

Crudden, Michael. *The Homeric Hymns*. Oxford: Oxford University Press, 2001.

Greer, John Michael. *The New Encyclopedia of the Occult*. Minnesota, Llewellyn Publications, 2003.

Homer. *The Iliad*. Translation by Peter Jones. Penguin Press, 2003.

Mellado, Carisa. *Mythic Oracle of the Ancient Greek Pantheon*. Blue Angel Publishing, 2008.

Opsopaus, John. *Guide to the Pythagorean Tarot*. St. Paul: Llewellyn Publications. 2001.

Orphic Hymns. *The Hymns of Orpheus*. Translation by Taylor, Thomas (1792). University of Pennsylvania Press, 1999.

Waite, Arthur Edward. *The Pictorial Key to the Tarot*. 1911. Last accessed: March 26, 2015. http://www.sacred-texts.com/tarot/pkt/

Images from WikiMedia Commons, unless otherwise noted. http://commons.wikimedia.org/

Made in the USA
Las Vegas, NV
14 December 2023

82593142R00066